THEN & NOW

CARROLLTON

Opposite: Photographer and insurance agent Benjamin M. Long, at right, was meeting his daughter, Frances, and granddaughter, Marion, at the Newnan train depot in this *c.* 1950 photograph. (Courtesy Benjamin M. Long Collection.)

THEN & NOW

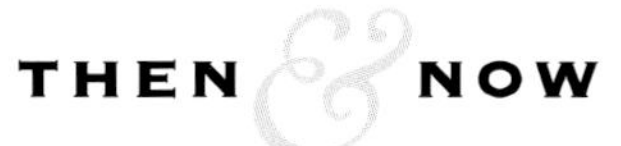

CARROLLTON

Suzanne K. Durham
and Emma Elaine Dobbs

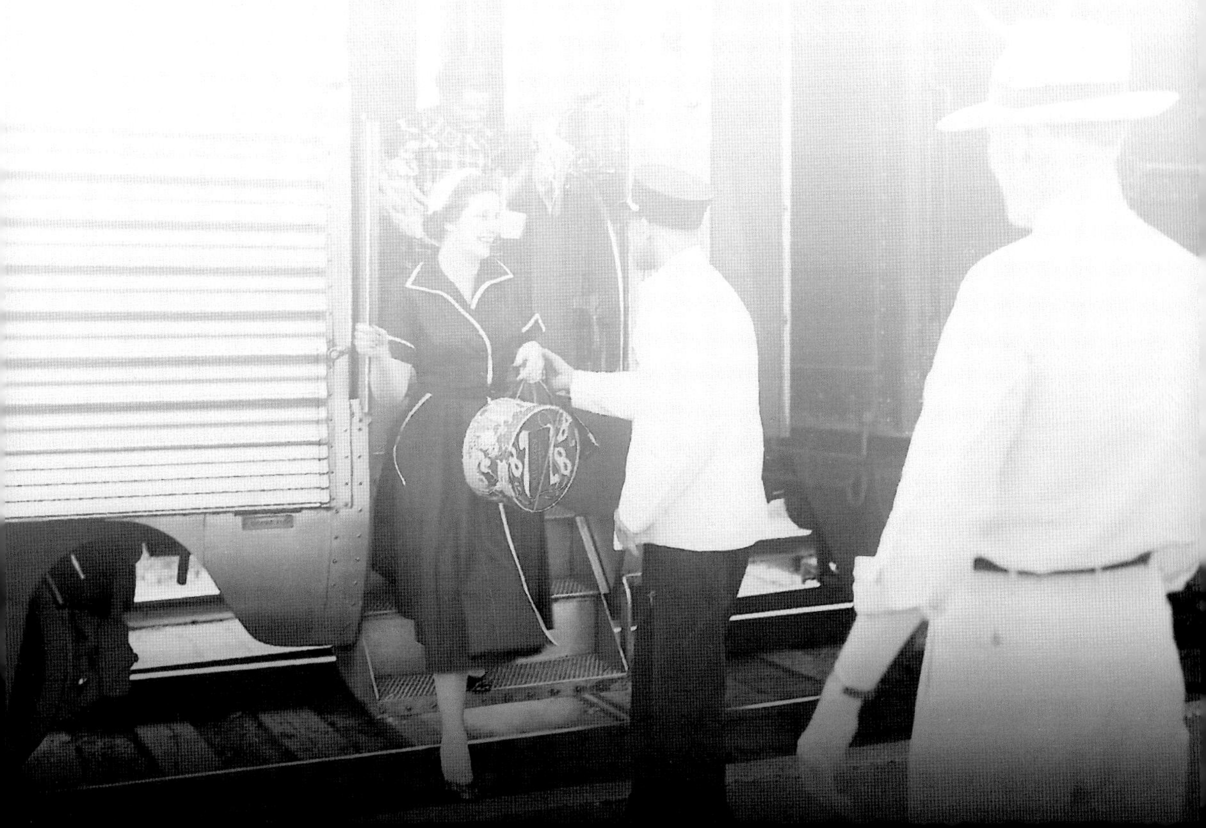

ISBN 978-0-7385-6646-7

Library of Congress Control Number: 2009930184

Published by Arcadia Publishing
Charleston, South Carolina

Printed in the United States of America

For all general information contact Arcadia Publishing at:
Telephone 843-853-2070
Fax 843-853-0044
E-mail sales@arcadiapublishing.com
For customer service and orders:
Toll-Free 1-888-313-2665

Visit us on the Internet at www.arcadiapublishing.com

On the Front Cover: L. C. "Cliff" Mandeville was one of Carrollton's original movers and shakers. He built this home on Maple Street in the late 19th century. Mandeville was responsible for much of Carrollton's early development, including the placement in Carrollton of the Fourth District A&M school, which has evolved into the University of West Georgia. He was a cotton and guano dealer, commercial developer, and the first president of the Mandeville Mills enterprises. The house has more recently been home to the Mansion restaurant and a catering business. (Then image courtesy Benjamin M. Long Collection; now image courtesy Emma Elaine Dobbs.)

On the Back Cover: Evangelist Gipsy Smith held a month-long revival in Carrollton in 1925 after several hundred townspeople built this tented tabernacle in one day. Local ladies provided basket dinners for the workingmen. The structure was located on Rome Street just north of the old city hall and had seating for 3,000. The revival was called "Carroll County for Christ." (Then image courtesy Benjamin M. Long Collection.)

Contents

ACKNOWLEDGMENTS

The vintage photographs that appear here were taken by Benjamin M. Long (1881–1973), whose collection was donated to the University of West Georgia's Ingram Library in 1993. Long was an amateur photographer who took pictures of many of Carrollton's buildings and houses for his insurance business, which he operated from 1917 until the 1960s. All of the modern photographs in this book were taken by Emma Elaine Dobbs, a photographer and recent art graduate of the University of West Georgia.

Much of the information accompanying these photographs was gleaned from Carrollton city directories, Sanborn Insurance maps, and histories of Carrollton published from 1910 to 1995.

Many thanks go to Lorene Flanders for her confidence in this project and to the Ingram Library faculty and staff for their support of the special collections, where these photographs are held. Special thanks to Perry Kirk for linking opportunity with talent. Extra-special thanks go to Daniel McMillan for providing his time and support to this project.

Introduction

Carrollton lies in the west-central region of Georgia, 45 miles due west of Atlanta and a few miles east of the Alabama state line. The "City Hospitable," as it was called in 1936, is the seat of Carroll County, established in December 1826. Carrollton was initially located several miles northeast of its present site when the county was much larger. With the formation of new counties out of Carroll, Carrollton was moved to its present location in order to be centrally located. The city square is still the hub of social, cultural, and commercial activity with numerous shops, restaurants, and galleries. Named for lawyer and congressman William C. Adamson (1854–1929), Adamson Square still is recognizable from its appearance 100 years ago. The city has been given two National Register district nominations—the South Carrollton Residential Historic District and, more recently, the Carrollton Downtown Historic District.

Its agricultural traditions made Carrollton a center of cotton production and transport by rail from the late 19th to the mid-20th century. The 1927 centennial slogan was "Where Small Farms Produce Big Crops." In 1906, an agricultural and mechanical school was established, which became a two-year teacher's college in 1933. Over the next 60 years, West Georgia College has become a state university and finally the University of West Georgia, with a current enrollment of more than 11,000 graduate and undergraduate students. Carrollton can claim Academy Award–winning actress Susan Hayward, who married Carrollton auto dealer Eaton Chalkley in 1957. Both are buried at Our Lady of Perpetual Help Catholic Church. Traffic engineering came to Carrollton in the 1950s when U.S. 27 (originally called Park Street) was made into the primary north-south highway, replacing Rome and Depot Streets as the main thoroughfares. However, because Carrollton is 8 miles from the closest interstate, the city's streets have not changed dramatically. Alabama Street, off the square, still takes you to Alabama.

This preserved quality of Carrollton is its charm. There appears to have been very little wholesale urban renewal. New construction tends to go up in piecemeal fashion, and adaptive reuse is common among many of Carrollton's buildings and houses. Many of these photographs feature commercial buildings and streetscapes that are easily recognizable today. The sleepy small town characteristics of Carrollton belie its future, however. The city and county have set a course to boost tourism, funding the restoration of the train depot and obtaining a commitment from the Georgia Quilt Council to locate a museum in Carrollton to interpret the region's mill and cotton history. We hope this book of photograph comparisons will give readers an appreciation for Carrollton's history as well as its future.

CHAPTER 1

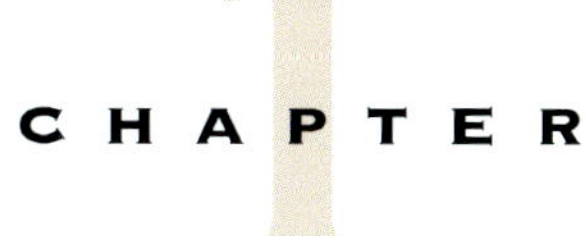

On the Square

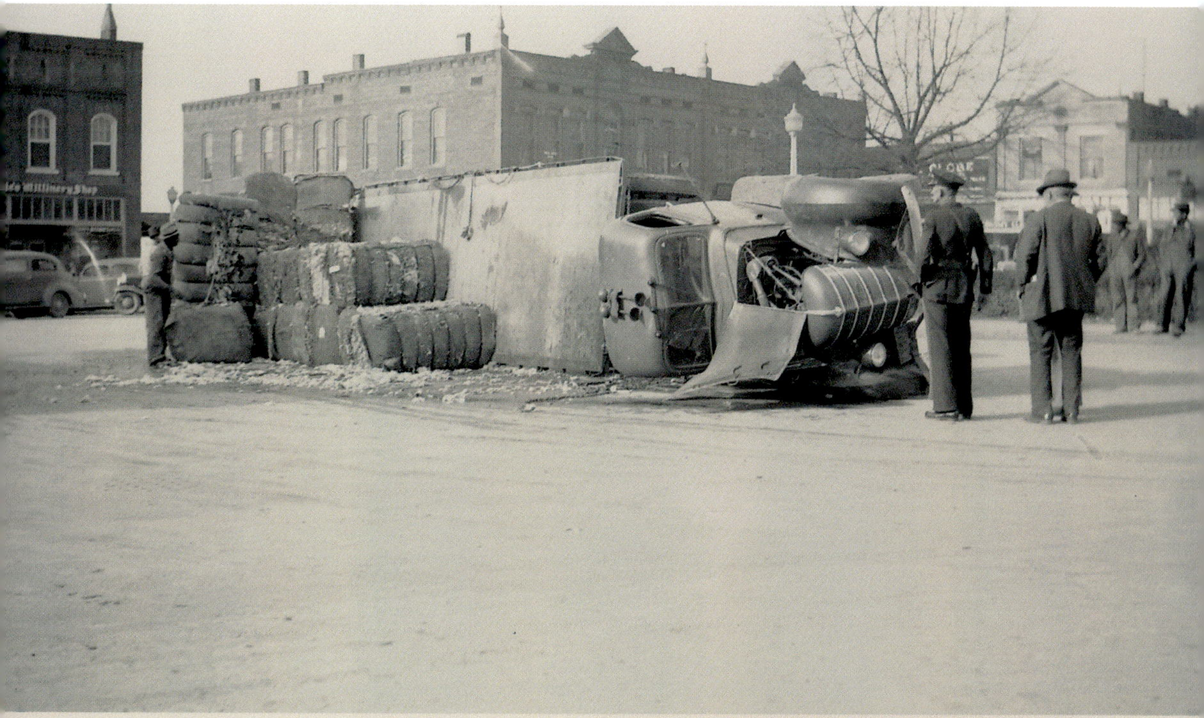

The Square. Perhaps this truck took the turn around Adamson Square too quickly and overturned, spilling its load of cotton bales. In the early 20th century, Carroll County led the state in cotton production, and cotton warehouses lined Bradley Street just south of the square. This photograph probably was taken *c.* 1930.

401 Adamson Square. Adamson Square is still the focal point of Carrollton's commercial and cultural activity. When this photograph was taken, probably in the 1930s, the square was a gathering spot with its parklike center island featuring a Confederate statue. The island was removed in 1958 to allow traffic to flow easily through the square. The People's Bank anchored the northwest corner of the square, though its top two floors have since been removed.

311 Adamson Square. This is a *c.* 1950 view looking west off the square at Alabama Street. The Griffin-New Pharmacy at left had a second location across from the new Tanner Hospital at the southern end of Dixie Street. Alabama Street was filled with shops and offices, including a five-and-dime, a billiard room, insurance agencies, and a shoe repair shop. On the right beyond the dime store was the city's bus depot.

301 Adamson Square. The square was fashioned around a center island where people could congregate in the shade of the trees to talk about the weather or politics. Traffic followed a roundabout pattern, and parking meters lined the sidewalks in front of the various department stores. The center island would disappear in 1958, but parking still lines the quadrants of the square, minus the parking meters.

301 Adamson Square SW. This 1950s photograph of the southwest quadrant of the square documents the square as the shopping center of Carrollton before malls came into existence. The 1956 City Directory lists five department stores on the square and another four stores just one block off the square. McGee's Bakery is still a downtown fixture, though it has had different locations over the years.

104 Adamson Square. At the time of this photograph, probably the early 1940s, the northeast quadrant of the square included McGee's Bakery on the corner, offices for attorneys Boykin and Boykin, Southern Bell Telephone and Telegraph, and the Georgia Power Company. Benjamin M. Long's insurance office was located above the Merrell and Company building, a clothing store that originally opened in 1904 as Merrell Brothers.

Demolition on the Square I. Like many small-town squares, Carrollton had a central park area featuring a Confederate monument and trees until 1958 when urban traffic engineering dictated the removal of this impediment to the flow of automobiles. This is a view looking southwest across the square as demolition began. The Confederate monument now stands in front of the county courthouse on Newnan Street.

Demolition on the Square II. Looking southeast across the square, this photograph shows a popular restaurant of the time, the Carroll Café. Before being named for local attorney and U.S. congressman W. C. Adamson, this geographical center of town was referred to as "Public Square." Adamson had a long career in Congress after holding office as city judge and city attorney in Carrollton.

Demolition on the Square III. The removal of the center island was nearly complete in this photograph. The base of the Confederate statue and a tree stump can be seen in the dirt. This view is looking northeast off the square down Newnan Street. The 1914 post office, now a professional building, can be seen in the distance. Benjamin M. Long's insurance office was located in the corner building with the Merrell clothing store.

404 Adamson Square. This view reflects the new traffic pattern across the square with a central traffic light and no center island. Probably taken soon after the construction in 1958, this photograph captures the northwest quadrant of the square, with the truck heading north onto Rome Street. Parking meters line the walks in front of a variety of stores, including Horton's Book Store, another fixture on the square said to be the oldest continuously operating bookstore in Georgia.

401 ADAMSON SQUARE. Another view looking northwest when the Peoples Bank still had four floors, this photograph probably was also taken soon after the redesign of the square in 1958. The bank building was shortened a few years ago in order to bring it more in line with the height of the other structures lining Adamson Square. The upper floors had housed professional offices for lawyers, insurance agencies, real estate companies, and physicians around the time of this photograph.

Insurance Adjusters. These business associates of Benjamin M. Long were posed in the northeast quadrant of Adamson Square, probably in the late 1950s, outside the building in which Long had his insurance office. The Johnson Drugs store is now the location of Miller's Restaurant, and the 5¢ to $1 store is the current location of the Classy Cricket gift shop. To the right, in what was a furniture and appliance store, there is now a restaurant.

This Side of the Tracks

430 Bradley Street. The Green Front Café was a fixture in Carrollton for over 50 years. The Green Front establishment changed hands several times, but kept the Green Front name, serving "Good Food—Well Prepared" at its location across from the train depot. This photograph was probably taken in the 1940s. The restaurant ceased operating about 1990, and the site is an empty lot now.

113 BRADLEY STREET. This 1940s view looking south from Adamson Square down Bradley Street is still recognizable today, though most of these storefronts have changed since then. Bradley Street was known for its warehouses and mills leading up to the train depot at its southernmost end. In this vintage photograph, the Lawler Mill is visible on the right with its many windows on the upper floor.

301 BRADLEY STREET. In 1939, the Lawler Hosiery Mills operated here, managed by Thomas J. Lawler. He was important as a founder of two local banks, a creamery, and a newspaper, in addition to serving as mayor in the 1940s. This building, photographed here in about 1960, was constructed in 1910 and is located next to the current Carrollton City Hall. In the mid-2000s, it was converted into loft-type condominiums.

315 Bradley Street. Located on the corner of Bradley and Center Streets, the Tabernacle Baptist Church was erected in 1913 with seating capacity for 1,400, the population of the entire city at that time. A new church was built on Cottage Hill Road in the 1980s, and the Bradley Street church was closed in 1989. A small park and the current Carrollton City Hall now occupy this site.

Central of Georgia Railway Station. This *c.* 1950 photograph of the train depot at the southern end of Bradley Street shows a building little changed over the years. It had fallen into disuse, but is now undergoing a restoration and renovation for use as a meeting center. The front portion contained the passenger waiting room and the office of the stationmaster. The large portion at the rear served as a warehouse for freight shipments.

401 Bradley Street. This house reflects the Steamboat Gothic Victorian–style of architecture popular from the 1880s to the 1900s. Built around 1900, its main feature was the use of decorative woodwork to make the house look like a riverboat. Steam-powered woodworking machinery allowed builders to create decorative woodwork in a fraction of the time it would take by hand. The house is located at the southwest corner of Bradley and Center Streets.

406 Bradley Street. This stately home was built about 1910 at the southeast corner of Bradley and Center Streets by local merchant and banker J. Thomas Bradley for whom the street is named. It has been the home for many years of the family of the late Tracy Stallings, former Carrollton mayor and state legislator who worked at the University of West Georgia as an administrator in development and public relations and as dean of students.

109 Lee Street. Carrollton Hardware Company had a store on Adamson Square beginning in 1900. This *c.* 1918 building is located next to the railroad tracks at the intersection of Bradley and Lee Streets and was used for storing the company's building materials. In 1981, the hardware company sold the building to sculptor Gordon Chandler, who owns it today. At left is Lee Street in this *c.* 1950 photograph.

122 Lee Street. This post Civil War–era house, photographed here *c.* 1950, was originally a residence. Now it houses a fine art frame dealer and county offices for substance-abuse treatment. A modern addition and a large asphalt parking lot have changed the building's look, but its original features are still visible. Originally called Austin Street, this section from Bradley to Dixie Streets changed names early in the 20th century.

205 Lee Street. Built in 1937, this former residence at the southeast corner of Tanner and Lee Streets now houses a financial planning company. In the early 1980s, it was converted from a residence into a dentist's office and has been used as medical offices and even a gift shop during the 1990s and early 2000s. Many of Carrollton's residential neighborhoods north and south of Newnan Street have been converted to professional offices without changing the look of the streetscape.

Croft Street Bridge. This structure was said to have been built in the late 19th century by the railroad company in order for Capt. James Croft's children to cross the tracks to attend church. Croft came to Carrollton to serve as conductor for the rail line between Carrollton and Griffin, Georgia. He built a house at 235 Croft Street. Though the bridge has been reinforced in modern times, it still closely resembles the older structure.

435 DIXIE STREET. This commercial building sits just north of the railroad tracks. It was built in 1882 and has had various uses. In 1922, it was an eight-car commercial garage. In this *c.* 1955 photograph, it housed the Jackson Brothers service garage. The building is currently vacant. The South Carrollton Residential Historic District ends just short of this structure.

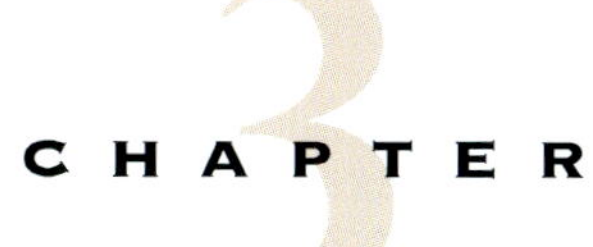

CHAPTER 3

OFF THE SQUARE

NEWNAN STREET. This 1957 photograph captured the view looking west toward the square down Newnan Street at the intersection with College Street. The Carroll Theatre at left was the local movie palace of the era. The car dealership at left was owned by Eaton Chalkley, better known as actress Susan Hayward's husband.

109 Newnan Street. Newnan Street, east off Adamson Square, retains the look of small storefronts today much as this 1950s photograph depicts. In this photograph, Worthy Drug Store, Folsom's Dress Shop, and the Carroll Café occupy three storefronts. In 1905, these buildings housed a confectionery, a meat store, and a grocery. In 1911, Citizens Bank occupied the corner building that is now a Merle Norman store.

323 Newnan Street The Carroll County Courthouse was built in 1929, probably not long before this photograph was taken from a point across the street where College Street intersects Newnan Street. A previous courthouse on this site was built in 1893. There were earlier courthouses in the center of Adamson Square built in the 1830s and then in 1857. Today renovations to the courthouse and an addition at the rear of the building are under way.

402 Newnan Street. The U.S. Post Office building was completed in 1914 on the site of the second Southland Hotel. The first Southland was built in 1891 on Alabama Street, but burned in 1901. Benjamin M. Long took this photograph of the post office in 1963. In the late 1960s, the county board of education occupied this building. Since the early 1990s, the building has housed attorney offices.

102 City Hall Avenue. The old city hall at the corner of Rome Street and City Hall Avenue is little changed from this 1960 photograph. Built in 1914, when the street was known as Smith Avenue, it contained most of the city offices, including the library. In the 1930s, it included the Works Progress Administration (WPA) sewing project in the basement. An auditorium was located on the second floor. Today the building houses offices for Southwire Company.

118 City Hall Avenue. In the 1950s when this photograph was taken, these commercial buildings were occupied, from left to right, by Smith Brothers Home Improvement Company, Bonner Radio and TV Shop, and the Atlanta Gas Light Company. In a nearly unchanged view, today's stores still are occupied by Smith Brothers Supply Company, selling plumbing fixtures. The Smith brothers' store was built around 1950.

City High School. The Carrollton Community Center in the first block of South White Street operates out of the old city high school, which was designed by renowned architect Neel Reid in the Georgian Revival style. The school was built in 1921 and used as a high school until 1962, when a new school was constructed off Oak Avenue. This building then served as the junior high school until the 1980s, when a junior high was built at the Oak Avenue complex.

205 Alabama Street. The Kroger supermarket occupied the building at the corner of Alabama and Cliff Streets, managed by Walter Herring. Barney Kroger opened his first store in Cincinnati in 1883, but the chain has become a standard supermarket in over 30 states. The vintage photograph was probably taken *c.* 1950. Today a vintage furniture store occupies the building.

310 Kramer Street. This neoclassical-style house, built in the late 19th century, was the home of German immigrant Ernest G. Kramer, an associate of L. C. Mandeville. Among other things, Kramer chartered a bank and telephone company in Carrollton and served as a vice president of Mandeville Mills. The house was moved here from its original location on South Street when U.S. 27 was constructed in the late 1950s.

226 Austin Avenue. Said to be the first brick dwelling in Carrollton, this house dates to the late 1870s and was labeled the Huckeba Place by Benjamin M. Long. It sits at the corner of Austin Avenue and Hill Drive, the latter a fairly new street, and has been renovated extensively so that much of the exterior detail has been removed. It is still a residence.

325 Stewart Street. This stately home was built in 1938 by former Carrollton mayor William Traylor, who also served on the board of education and was vice president of the Carrollton Federal Savings and Loan. Traylor also owned a feed mill store and a hardware store. The architecture borrows from the English Cottage style that was popular from the 1920s to the 1940s.

516 Longview Street. It is interesting to compare the changes made to this 1890s house at the corner of Longview and Carroll Streets. The earlier photograph dates to the 1950s and shows changes already made in the form of an exterior staircase, indicating conversion to apartments on the second story. In the vintage photograph, there are no chimneys visible, but the original house must have had at least one.

207 South Tanner Street. The Carroll Masons Lodge No. 69 was built in 1931 at the corner of South Tanner and Mill Streets. It remains little changed today. The vintage photograph shows warehouses to the north and the backs of the buildings that front on Newnan Street. A county courthouse annex is under construction now just north of this location.

516 Cedar Street. This excellent example of Victorian Gothic–style architecture is undergoing a restoration after a number of years of neglect. The house was built in 1887 and was known as the Brown Home place. Currently, it goes by the name Palm Villa. In 1957, when this photograph was taken, the house was owned by local physician Dr. Phillip Astin. The lot is extremely deep and wide, extending north nearly to Sims Street.

414 College Street. As with many of Carrollton's former residences, this 1891 house has been converted to professional offices. Formerly known as the Aderhold House, it is located across from the site of the old College Street School that served for many years as one of Carrollton's public schools after the turn of the century. That block now contains a Carroll County government building, which occupies a former elementary school that had replaced the old College Street school.

219 Chandler Street. This home at the corner of North Cliff Street is undergoing renovation, though it still resembles the house as pictured in the 1950s. Built in 1881, it is an example of the L-shaped Victorian style that was popular at the turn of the century. At one time, the house was occupied by city police chief Wiley Garrett. This street was named for Thomas Chandler, said to be Carrollton's first lawyer.

Our Lady of Perpetual Help. This Catholic church was established in 1961 with money and land donated by actress Susan Hayward and her husband, Carrollton car dealer Eaton Chalkley. The couple owned a farm off Temple Road northeast of Carrollton, and they are buried at the church. The church had used a former Episcopal chapel at the corner of White Street and West Avenue during the 1950s. The BB&T parking deck is located on that site now.

Tanner Lake. In 1954, local businessman John Tanner opened a recreational beach on a man-made lake in western Carroll County called the Beach at Lakeview. It is said he had 22 boxcars of sand brought in from Florida to create the beach. Later it was called Tanner's Beach, and in 1970 the state purchased the property and named it John Tanner State Park. In 2010, Carroll County took over the park and its operations from the state.

CHAPTER 4

Historic Dixie Street

110 Dixie Street. Carrollton Federal Savings and Loan operated at this location next to the First Baptist Church. Built in 1956, it was the site of the old Hotel Crepe Myrtle. In 1980, the property was sold to Community First Bank, which built a BB&T bank at this location, later adding an office building and parking structure.

119 Dixie Street. Local businessman John Tanner lived in this craftsman-style house around the time this photograph was taken in the mid-20th century. Tanner was a president and manager of the C. M. Tanner wholesale grocery company on Maple Street. He was responsible for creating what is now Tanner State Park in western Carroll County. The house to the right is gone, replaced with a parking lot.

205 Dixie Street. This house is an excellent example of the Victorian Gothic style, which was fashionable after the Civil War. It was built by John K. Redwine, a bookkeeper for Mandeville Mills, around 1890. Redwine was the grandson of Sanford Kingsbery, a Vermont native who came to Carrollton in 1830. Kingsbery was the original owner of the lot on the square where the Peoples Bank was later built.

215 Dixie Street. Local attorney Earl Staples, active in the Carrollton Junior Chamber of Commerce, lived here in 1956. The house was built in 1902 and has remained a residence. This cottage-style architecture was popular from the 1880s to the 1910s. The northern half of Dixie Street lies within the South Carrollton Residential Historic District, which is listed on the National Register of Historic Places.

216 Dixie Street. This house is an example of the craftsman cottage style that was popular from the 1910s to the 1930s. Typical is the high-hipped roof with a central dormer window. The roof design allowed hot air to rise, letting cooler air fill the rooms. James Crowley, an inspector with the Veterans Administration, resided here in 1956. It is still a residence today.

220 Dixie Street. An example of building infill in a much older neighborhood, this house was constructed in 1958 just north of 224 Dixie Street. On the National Register nomination for the historic district, this house is noted as an intrusion along with a modern apartment complex and several other ranch-style houses. It is interesting that the same four rocking chairs are currently on the front porch.

224 Dixie Street. This photograph was taken from the front walk of Benjamin M. Long's home at 301 Dixie Street, probably around 1945 based on the car across the street. The little girl is Long's granddaughter, Marion, who was born in 1942. Much of Dixie Street's residential section is unchanged from the early 20th century except for modern infill on previously empty lots.

301 Dixie Street. This excellent and well-preserved example of a craftsman-style home was built in 1914 by the photographer, Benjamin M. Long. It is occupied currently by only its second owners, who purchased the house in 1979. Long and his wife, Helen, raised their two daughters here. Long operated an insurance business in Carrollton from 1917 until he retired in the 1960s.

302 Dixie Street. This home was built in 1900 by local attorney Sidney Holderness. It was later owned by Brooks O. Pittman, a West Georgia College instructor who died unexpectedly in 1952 at age 48. His widow, Margaret, lived here around the time of this photograph. She was a librarian in Bowdon, Georgia. The Pittman family still owns the house.

305 Dixie Street. This home was built in 1902 in the neoclassical style, meant to hark back to the look of the antebellum Southern mansion. Around the time of this old photograph, the home was owned by physician Davis Reese, who had an office on the fourth floor of the Peoples Bank building on Adamson Square. Many of Carrollton's prominent leaders and middle-class citizens lived in the Dixie Street neighborhood.

315 Dixie Street. Attorney Shirley C. Boykin lived in this house at the corner of Dixie and Austin Streets. He was Benjamin M. Long's brother-in-law, having married Long's sister, Helen, in 1913. Boykin and his brother, Buford, owned the law firm Boykin and Boykin, which had offices on Adamson Square. The house was built about 1900 and reflects the Queen Anne Victorian style.

401 Dixie Street. Built in 1912, this house was owned by Walter Beck at about the time this Long photograph was taken, *c.* 1955. Beck owned the Pontiac and GMC dealership on North Tanner Street. The Queen Anne style of architecture was popular from the 1880s to the early 1900s. The landscaping on this portion of Dixie Street reflects the informal, naturalistic style of plantings favored during the late 19th and early 20th centuries.

415 Dixie Street. This cottage-style house was built in 1900 as a residence and remained so until recent times. A new street, History Drive, was built next to it, creating a corner lot. Luna Cook, who worked at the C. M. Tanner wholesale grocery company, lived here in 1956. The house is now used as a professional building for family counseling, hypnotherapy, and massage therapy.

710 Dixie Street. Constructed in 1950, this building originally was used by the Griffin-New Pharmacy, which also had a location on Adamson Square. Anderson's Florist used part of the building. Both stores were located conveniently to the new Tanner Memorial Hospital, which was opened across the street in 1949. Today this building is barely recognizable, now housing the Tanner Hospice Care program.

CHAPTER 5

NORTH OF THE SQUARE

LOOKING NORTH. Down Rome Street off Adamson Square, this 1961 photograph shows the signage for drivers headed to Bremen and Rome, Georgia. By the time of this photograph, the widening of U.S. 27 through Carrollton would have been complete. Rome Street connects with U.S. 27 about a mile north of this point. The young woman is Marion McNamara, graddaughter of the photographer.

View down Rome Street. This view of Rome Street looking north in the early 1950s shows it to be a commercial thoroughfare. Note the location of Horton's bookstore, said to be the oldest continuously operating bookstore in the state of Georgia. Much of the streetscape on the west side of the street is intact today, though the occupants of these storefronts have changed.

302 Rome Street. The northwest corner of Rome Street and Johnson Avenue has changed dramatically since Coalson's Army Store and Daniel Furniture store occupied this site in the 1950s. In 1939, this was the location of a grocery company. This vintage photograph was taken in 1958. Today the modern buildings are owned by Southwire Company.

320 Rome Street. Back in the good old days, new tires only cost $9.95 each. This 1960s photograph shows the OK Tire Store whose basic structure is visible today, though the stylized OK sign is gone. The *c.* 1961 building has housed a tire dealer since the 1970s. Back in the 1950s, this was a used car lot.

401 Rome Street. Colonial grocery stores were common throughout the Southeast, having originated in Norfolk, Virginia, in 1901. In 1940, the Colonial chain was headquartered in Atlanta. This store was just opening, probably in the early 1960s, on the east side of Rome Street. Earlier, there was a Colonial store located in the northwest quadrant of Adamson Square. Today this block of Rome Street has been expanded and recently renovated.

402 Rome Street. In the 1950s, Georgia Power Company and Southern Bell Telephone and Telegraph occupied these two buildings on the west side of Rome Street. At that time, customers could buy appliances or get appliances repaired at the store. Though much renovated, both buildings are recognizable today. They are used as professional and government offices.

504 Rome Street. This 19th-century house has been called the oldest house in Carrollton. It has undergone several changes, such as enclosing the second-story porch and part of the first-story porch. In the early and middle part of the 20th century, it was occupied by R. Alton Lane, who owned a local truck and tractor company and served on city council. Today it still serves as a residence and faces east towards the "401" plaza.

608 Rome Street. Horace Cole, president of Carroll Realty and Insurance, owned this home in the mid-1950s when this photograph was taken. Built in 1892, the home was typical of the Queen Anne Victorian style of architecture popular from the 1880s to 1900s. In 1939, it was owned by Charles Walker, the president of the Peoples Bank. The house remains little changed today.

705 Rome Street. This neoclassical-style house was built in 1898 and served as an apartment house in the 1930s. It is located across from the Neva Lomason Memorial Public Library and is occupied by dental offices today. At one time, Annie Belle Weaver, the first librarian at West Georgia College, was a tenant here. Weaver served as college librarian for more than 30 years before retiring in the late 1960s.

708 Rome Street. This house sat on the site where the public library is today. The hipped-style cottage was built *c.* 1910 near the corner of Rome and Spring Streets. In 1939, it was the home of Marion Fisher, a member of the board of education and vice president of Carrollton Federal Savings and Loan. By the mid-1950s, it was owned by James Griffin, owner of Griffins Department Store. The library was built on this site in 1967.

805 Rome Street. This *c.* 1940 house was occupied for many years by Carrollton attorney Reuben Word and his wife, Mary Florence Word. Mary has been a professional genealogist and active in the Carroll County Genealogical and Historical societies for many years. The house has undergone some renovations and additions, but retains its original appearance.

936 Rome Street. This Victorian cottage was built in the postbellum period and has retained its original look. In the early to mid-20th century, it was owned by A.L. Bonner, who operated Bonner's Grocery on Alabama Street. By 1980, it was owned by Kenneth Farmer, a city recreation director. Today it is still a residence.

1104 Rome Street. This craftsman-style cottage at the corner of Rome and Williams Streets is virtually unchanged in appearance today. With its deep, overhanging eaves, exposed decorative brackets, and mixed materials of stone and wood, the house is an excellent example of the early-20th-century architecture style. In 1939, it was occupied by George Burnett, an insurance agent for Massachusetts Mutual. By 1956, it was owned by Allen Meeks, who operated Meeks Motor Company.

1141 Rome Street. The original house "Oak Lawn" was built prior to the Civil War by Sanford Kingsbery, a New Englander who brought his family to Carrollton in 1830 and established a mercantile and milling business in the fledgling town of Carrollton. This 1950s photograph shows 20th-century additions to the home. Kingsbery raised racehorses and had a racetrack on his estate. Today the house is an inn and reception center.

CHAPTER 6

OUT TO THE COLLEGE

233 MAPLE STREET. This Amoco station was erected in the late 1920s at the northeast corner of Maple Street and what was then known as South Park Street. Park Street was enlarged to what is now U.S. Highway 27 in the late 1950s. Today an automated car wash is located at this corner.

120 Alabama Street. This 1950s view is looking southwest toward the University of West Georgia where Maple Street runs diagonally off Alabama Street. On the street sign, "The Beach" referred to John Tanner's park in western Carroll County with man-made lakes and a sand beach. Many small storefronts populated this triangular block, which featured department stores such as Griffin's, shown here, and a Belks-Rhodes store located behind the photographer.

119 Maple Street. Hotel Carrollton advertised its moderate rates, excellent food, convenience, and real hospitality in 1956, probably around the time this photograph was taken. The building, located across from Carrollton Presbyterian Church, was constructed in 1911 and operated as the Clifton Hotel prior to the time depicted here. It has undergone another face-lift and is used today as an office building by United Community Bank.

327 Maple Street. This street scene from the 1950s is very similar to today's view, though this house's occupants now look at a modern gas station across Maple Street. When Park Street was made into a four-lane highway (U.S. 27) in the late 1950s, the adjacent blocks, such as this one, became more commercialized. This was one of many Carrollton homes built at the end of the 19th century by the brothers Samuel, William, and Joseph Gaston.

334 Maple Street. The so-called Camp-Bickford House was built in the 1890s by Dr. J. C. Brown. He exchanged houses in 1899 with his son-in-law, Dr. J. B. Camp, of Whitesburg, Georgia. Originally, there was a turret roof over the second-story room on the left. Mrs. J. B. Camp had it removed, as reflected in the 1950s photograph here. A more recent renovation has restored the turret.

338 Maple Street. This was the home of J. Appleton Mandeville whose father, L. C. "Cliff" Mandeville, had begun the Mandeville Mills enterprises and many other business and educational ventures that resulted in Carrollton's dramatic turn-of-the-century growth. The elder Mandeville's home was across the street from this house, which was built around 1910. J. A. Mandeville was involved in managing his father's businesses as well as real estate and insurance businesses.

402 Maple Street. This 1920s house at the corner of Maple and South Aycock Streets was home to the Pi Kappa Phi fraternity until 2009 when the fraternity relocated to the Greek Village at the University of West Georgia. The house is virtually unchanged on the exterior from its original appearance as a private residence. In 1956, approximately the time when this photograph was taken, it was occupied by a machinist named Carlos Wynn.

408 Maple Street. This 1950s photograph shows the Joseph Aycock house, built *c.* 1862 and owned by one of Carrollton's leading industrialists who started Mandeville Mills with L. C. Mandeville in 1902. The house is situated next to the railroad tracks that cross Maple Street. Aycock built the first modern cotton ginnery in Carrollton, was a member of the state legislature, and organized the Carrollton Oil Mills. This building now houses a general contracting restoration firm.

409 Maple Street. In 1939, about 10 years before this photograph was taken, Drake Motor Company was located on Alabama Street. Judging from the vintage of the vehicles, this photograph was probably taken in the late 1940s. By the 1950s, this site was used by the Head Ford Company. Today the building houses the Music Depot, a musical instrument dealer. The showroom and glass-block detail over the doorway are unchanged.

506 Maple Street. The Maryon Hosiery Mill, originally located on Bradley Street, made fine hosiery for boys at this plant. The company president was Theodor "Ted" F. Hirsch, a German immigrant who was Carrollton's mayor from 1972 to 1974, and who also served as a financial officer for the University of West Georgia. By 1976, the mill, named for Hirsch's wife, no longer operated here.

519 Maple Street. Using the water tower as a point of reference, it is apparent that this block of commercial buildings where Longview Avenue intersects with Maple Street has been torn down. Even the traffic light that used to hang at this intersection is gone. Lonn Wessinger operated this grocery *c.* 1956. He lived at 439 Longview Avenue. The Maple Street School, one of Carrollton's original public schools, was located just west of this site.

701 Maple Street. This neoclassical mansion was built in 1907 by H. O. Lovvorn, who was appointed secretary and treasurer of Mandeville Mills after Joseph Aycock's early death in 1910. Lovvorn later became vice president of the mill enterprise. His widow, Effie, was still living in this house in 1956. It is located at the corner of Maple Street and Lovvorn Road. Today it is still a residence.

833 Maple Street. This beautiful example of the art deco architectural style at the northeast corner of Maple and Matthew Streets was probably constructed in the 1930s, when the style was popular. According to the 1922 Sanborn Insurance map, there were no buildings at this location at that time. Today a BP service station, constructed in 1986, operates at the same site, though with not nearly the same architectural aesthetic appeal.

1601 Maple Street. The Bonner House was built in 1844 by Thomas Bonner, who owned a cotton plantation on the site of what is now the University of West Georgia. The house was moved in 1913 several hundred yards east from its original site. It served as the first women's dormitory for the college. Today it houses offices for student activities at UWG. This vintage photograph was probably taken in the 1960s.

1601 Maple Street. This Episcopal Church was built in 1893 at the corner of West Avenue and White Street. In 1953, the building was sold to Our Lady of Perpetual Help Catholic Church, which later gave the structure to the University of West Georgia in 1964. The old structure was moved to the UWG campus and dedicated as the interfaith Kennedy Chapel by Robert Kennedy in memory of his brother, Pres. John Kennedy, who had been assassinated in 1963.